Memories of Monday

A lighthearted account of Washday
as seen through the eyes of many
who laboured before the days of
washing machines

by

Joan Pearson

Retired Senior Lecturer in Home Economics
at Northern Counties College
(now part of Newcastle upon Tyne Polytechnic)

Illustrations by Diane E. Robertson

WILLIAM SESSIONS LIMITED
THE EBOR PRESS, YORK
ENGLAND

ISBN 1 85072 053 3

The front cover shows the Poss-Stick and
Dolly Tub described on page 16 in Chapter IV

Printed by
William Sessions Limited
The Ebor Press, York,
England

Contents

Work apace, apace, apace,
Honest labour wears a lovely face.

T. Dekker

Introduction

Eating, drinking, living and loving are part of life as is washing, whether self or clothes. Why choose to write about something as mundane as washing? To answer the question, it is not I who write, it is the people who have written to me with their descriptions and their grandmothers' accounts and memories of Monday.

The idea for a book came whilst taking parties of visitors round the Victorian laundry of one of Yorkshire's National Trust houses – Beningbrough Hall. Their tales of the washing ways of other days so stimulated my interest that I kept notes of what people told me, and then hit on the idea of writing to various groups, such as the W.I., asking for further material. The response was excellent and this book is the result. I have kept to the period between 1830 and 1930.

CHAPTER I

Washing
(19th century – early 20th century)

Wash on Monday – you've all the week to dry

IT IS HARD FOR THE PRESENT GENERATION to conceive of a time when there were no electric washing machines, spin driers, launderettes or packets of detergents – a time when washing was not a matter of pushing clothes into a machine, selecting the washing programme by turning a switch, then pressing a button and leaving the machine to do the work. Between 1830 and 1930 there were changes in washing methods but these only came gradually and for the most part it was a back-breaking job. In poor families, the burden fell on the housewife helped by the female members of her family.

Mrs Beeton suggests that in those households where one servant alone was kept, the washing should be sent out, but in a household employing both cook and housemaid the work should be divided between them. Cook should do the coarser and heavier things, the housemaid the finer and all the starching and ironing. Some such households employed a washerwoman like 'Sarah our washerwoman who arrived always looking spick and span, smiling and rosy-cheeked after the mile walk from her widow's cottage'. Jenny the town washerwoman was much less appealing: she wore a black dress with a heavy apron of coarse sacking and skewered to her head at a rakish angle was a man's cloth cap. In the big houses of course there would be laundrymaids who were fully occupied keeping the household linen clean.

From the middle of the nineteenth century up to the 1914–18 war, washing was not done at any time as is often the case today. It was a planned campaign which could take place weekly, fortnightly, monthly or even quarterly. In fact, your social station could be assessed by the frequency of your washing. The poor, having fewer clothes, would wash more frequently than those better off. Even today I have spoken with two old ladies who told me that when one of their three aunts died, the others

1

decided solemnly that they would change a lifelong habit and wash once a month, instead of once in two months, as they had done formerly.

In his *Book of the Home,* a practical guide to household management written in 1905, Hugh Colman Davidson points out that

> . . . the old-fashioned plan, which still exists in country districts and on the Continent, of allowing the linen to accumulate for a long period and then devoting weeks to the washing, is one that cannot be too strongly condemned. Dust and disease are synonymous terms, and however we may ignore it or alter its title, soiled linen is dirty linen and the sooner it is clean linen the better for all concerned. A fortnight is long enough to defer washing, and those are better off who can arrange it weekly.

Old customs die hard, as I found in the early 30's when I stayed for some months in a small provincial town, in what is now East Germany. During that time there was one Grosse Wäsche only. The whole affair was organised with true Germanic thoroughness and a woman was employed to help for three days. To my astonishment, dozens of dirty white cotton clothes were brought from their hiding place in the attic. These were marshalled into piles and soaked, washed and boiled etc., until ready to be hung on lines set up for the purpose on a piece of common ground at the back of the house. Everything had to be in its correct place – there were rows of towels, rows of pillowcases, pants and petticoats, no garment hanging in a cheerful haphazard fashion away from its peers. White sheets and tablecloths lay chastely on the grass, while a solemn hausfrau sprinkled them with cold water from a watering can to aid bleaching in the sun.

My clothes were not allowed to join them. They had caused a sensation as they were coloured and scanty by comparison with the wide whites. In fact, when they were washed, which was frequently as I hadn't enough to keep going for three months, people paraded by to take a furtive peep at them.

Just as a matter of interest, the girls I met then would proudly show me the embroidered sheets and towels collected for their trousseaux and were horrified to learn that I had nothing.

A German friend sent me the following account of the Grosse Wäsche in her home which bears out my own observations.

> In my early childhood – before the first war – this was a tremendous institution. It took place every Monday in all German households. Linen was used lavishly – in my home sheets and pillowcases were changed *every day* – there was a different tablecloth for breakfast, lunch (mittagessen) which was mostly the main meal, and a lighter meal at night (abendessen). Bath robes, towels and kitchen towels were also frequently changed, particularly the ones for drying glass and silver. For all this a truly Grosse Wäsche assembled each week.

In my own case, the maid on duty on Sunday (we had two maids who were free alternately on Sundays) soaked all washing in big wooden tubs on Sunday night (naturally whites and coloureds apart). She also lit the big coal-fired iron boiler and certain things were slowly boiled overnight. We lived in a sixteenth century house where a former barn had been made into a large laundry. There was a big wooden 'pin' used for turning the washing in the hot boiler; also of course, scrubbing boards. Soaking was done with braune Seife, a soft yellowish soap, the stuff rubbed later with hard soap. Washing-blue was used. Most linen and damask was carefully starched and flat irons were heated on the big kitchen stove. In summer drying was done on a bleaching field at the edge of the town which was rented out to families on an annual basis – certain hours. There was a wooden hut with a big Mangel – a huge wringer – and sheets in particular were spread on the grass for bleaching after having been rinsed in a passing stream. The 'lower classes' took all their washing to the river for rinsing, some even did their whole washing there. (I have seen Berber women in North Africa do that only a few years ago). In winter, washing was finished at home. We had a smaller version of the Mangel – and it was then dried in the attics on lines fixed from rafter to rafter. Linen was always conveyed from place to place in wicker baskets – to the bleaching fields on a small cart drawn by the maids and also up the many stairs to the attics. It was the task of the ironing maids to sort out anything which needed mending (new buttons etc.) and attend to this the following afternoon.

Most households – including our own – engaged a special Waschfrau to help on Mondays on an hourly basis. They were paid by the hour and had their meals, often bringing a small child with them.

People spoke of washing their 'linen' – meaning sheets, tablecloths, shirts etc., but other materials were involved, mostly cotton, wool and silk. These are still with us, but methods have been discovered of treating the materials to make washing easier and in addition are the many man-made fibres which are quickly washed and dried.

Coloured materials that had been printed or dyed often required individual treatment, as early dyes were not reliable and tended to run easily. Housewives and laundresses had their own favourite recipes for the treatment of such fabrics. Washing was not only hard labour, it was in some cases a skilled art.

Perhaps that is why Peggoty, in the *Girls Own Paper* (1884) 'had better send her red flannel and washleather bodice to a cleaner, to be renovated by the new cleaning process in which no wetting is required. She will be sure to spoil it at home!'

CHAPTER II

Water and Soap

Wash on Tuesday – you're no far by

Water

WASHING CANNOT BE DONE WITHOUT WATER. It will come as a surprise to today's young to learn that in the middle of the nineteenth century water was not piped into houses as a matter of course. In the country, water for the washing was collected in buckets from rivers, streams, ponds, wells and pumps. Cottages and farms had rain-water butts for collecting the water, which was much prized being soft. Even in the twentieth century, farmers' wives and countrywomen have written to me saying:–

> . . . water for *everything* was in a tap outside the back door.
> . . . the water was carried from a 500 gallon tank outside, which collected the rain-water off the farm building. The tank had a brass tap at the bottom.
> . . . three cottages shared a stand-pipe. Mother kept the key for this so that the children could not turn it on and so waste water.

In the Highlands and Islands even today, some heavier items such as rag-rugs are held down in streams by stones. The fast moving currents wash away the winter's dirt.

The towns had a water supply of sorts, though this was very much a local concern. For example, in York many houses had their own wells which left much to be desired, often being sited near cess-pits and other undesirable places. Up until 1846 water was also pumped from the River Ouse and supplied direct to various lucky houses in the City *without filtration*. Roughly 5860 houses received this water, but not all the time on tap, as it were. One half of the town had water on Monday, Wednesday and Friday, the other half on Tuesday, Thursday and Saturday. There was no supply on Sunday. It is said that those houses which had water, stored it in two large pots, according to the quantity required. The water was allowed to settle for a day or two before using. One shudders to think of the debris found at the bottom of these pots.

4

By the 1930's, however, things had much improved and over 30,000 houses were receiving treated water daily. It is only during times of drought, or during strikes which may effect water supplies, that the majority of people in this country have any conception of what life is like without a constant supply of water.

Soap

In England, soap had been taxed since the time of Charles I: only the rich could afford to buy it. The poor made do with nothing or such herbs that were at hand. Conditions in towns during the nineteenth century were dreadful, and it was only when a terrible cholera epidemic broke out in 1848 that Gladstone repealed the tax on soap and a programme was started of health and hygiene reform.

On farms and in cottages it was common enough to make soap. The following rather primitive recipe for a common scrubbing soap was used by a farmer's wife in Yorkshire:

> 6½ pounds of rendered fat
> 1 pound of caustic soda
> 3 pints water

Dissolve the caustic soda in the water until it becomes hot. Leave until warm. Melt the rendered fat and have it warm. Pour the fat slowly into the soda and stir with an iron spoon till mixed. Line a wooden box with damp calico. Pour in the mixture, cover and put into a warm place until next day. Cut into bars and leave for at least one month before using.

The scraps of fat were collected over a period of time and consequently some of these soaps could have rather an odd smell. Home-made toilet soap would substitute coconut oil and a little glycerine for some of the clarified fat, and perfume might also be added.

A soap-cutter, like a miniature guillotine, was a useful kitchen gadget for chopping the hardened soap into smaller, more usable pieces. Two books in my possession, both produced by Lever Brothers – *The Sunlight Year Book* (1897) and *Womans World* (1901) contain chapters on washing at home. Naturally they extol the virtues of Sunlight Soap. One has a cheerful little song to the tune of *The lass of Richmond Hill*:

On Richmond Hill there lives a lass
More bright than May-day morn,
Her clothes all other folk's surpass
When they the line adorn.
This lass so neat with smiles so sweet
Has won my right good will,
Because she uses SUNLIGHT SOAP
Sweet lass of Richmond Hill.

The television jingle is no new thing!!

By 1863 a fairly crude soap-powder was being produced. In 1900 came the first soap-flakes. Firms such as Proctor and Gamble had improved soap-making enormously by 1940, but it was to be another ten years before the detergent as we know it came into being.

wash house

CHAPTER III

The Washhouse

Wash on Wednesday — much about the same

THE WASHHOUSE EVOLVED FROM THE BOILER. Originally, water for the washing was heated in a large pan or cauldron over the hearth fire. Later the cauldron was stood outside supported by bricks with a fire underneath and finally came a free-standing boiler with its own built-in fire. The washing itself was done outside, weather permitting. It is easy to see why the boiler had at first a rough shelter built over it, and then came the stone or brick-built washhouse where all the equipment needed was stored. One such mentioned to me stood for many years at the back of a row of cottages to be shared by all. There was no water laid on but it was fetched from a communal tap at the end of the row. Competition was keen to book the washhouse for Monday and of course the strongest and toughest character won.

By the end of the nineteenth century, town houses had washhouses in their yards or a copper was built in next to the range or bricked in, in the corner of the scullery, the washing being done there at the shallow sink or slickenstone.

For those houses too poor to have a washhouse, the public washhouse was a great boon. The following extract from a lecture given by Charles Larkin M.R.C.S.L. to the inhabitants of Gateshead on 13th October 1855, stated what was available:

> The earliest public washhouse was after the first visitation of cholera when a Liverpool housewife charged neighbours for boiling clothes. Eighty-five families made use of this facility for 1d. per week for the accommodation.

Following this venture the Liverpool Authority built their first public baths and washhouses which were opened on 28th May 1842. Newcastle upon Tyne and Gateshead followed this lead in 1855. The facilities provided for washing included duckboards to keep the feet dry, a washing

7

tub, boiling tub and rinsing tub. Boiling was done by injecting steam. Hot and cold water was on tap, emptying was by drainage plug. Wringing was done by a machine abstracting water by centrifugal force. A poss tub was also provided with a sink at floor level for drainage. There was a ledge to brush or beat the clothes and thirty or forty 'horses',– sliding frames of galvanised iron, for drying. These frames could be drawn in and out of air heated cupboards to speed up the process.

The laundry was furnished with two patent mangles, a stove for heating irons and tables covered with blankets for ironing clothes.

With these facilities washing, drying, mangling and ironing could all be done in the course of a few hours.

In the six months ending 28th August 1855, 3,597 persons used the washhouses, washing hours totalling 15,464, an average of 140 persons per week.

These washhouses were a cheerful meeting place for the locals – perhaps this is why a Mr Hamilton who wrote a book on *Household Management for the Labouring Classes* says rather sadly: 'I have heard it said that most of the gossip of a place springs from round the washing tubs'.

Large houses such as Beningbrough Hall in Yorkshire, Pakenham Hall in Ireland, Erdigg in Wales and many others had their own laundries. There would be plenty of work for them as a vast amount of linen was used daily in such establishments. The laundries were situated well away from the main body of the house as the laundry, when in use, caused a good deal of bustle, clouds of steam and an all pervasive smell of washing! Also, easy access to a drying yard or green was essential.

In Scotland, although the large houses built by the jute manufacturers were not halls, even they had a laundry room and a bleaching green was regarded as a necessity. The private laundry consisted of two, sometimes three, rooms: one for the actual washing and the others for drying, ironing and airing the linen.

At Beningbrough Hall the laundry appears to have run true to form, as it was situated in a group of buildings well away from the house. There are two separate rooms, one for washing and one for drying and ironing the clothes. The washing room has a high ceiling and is well lit with two long windows. These would also be useful for ventilation, although ventilation bricks also helped with this. On one wall are two huge coppers, which have to be reached by steps. A pump supplied the water for the larger of the two coppers, presumably the second was filled by scooping water from the first. Both coppers had their own fire, no doubt well supplied with wood from the grounds. One copper would be used for boiling the clothes and the second for the water needed to wash and rinse them.

On the opposite wall stands a row of six wooden sinks, each served by a cold water tap. These sinks discharged into a single drain set in the floor and as the floor is stone and slopes slightly towards the drain, any water spilt from tubs or coppers would run easily into it. Any other equipment would have consisted of movable items such as tubs, dollies and possers.

The drying rooms had a fire both for drying the clothes and heating the irons. There were no heated driers, but two giant racks were suspended from the ceiling by a network of chains radiating from the pulley. The weight of these filled with wet clothes must have been enormous. At least two or more laundresses would have been needed to raise them.

As in the washhouse, the room is well lit by three long windows under which were the sturdy tables, just the right height for the ironing. Here, too, the stone floor must have proved hard on the feet.

The other equipment such as clothes horses, flat irons, standing irons and goffering tongs would all have their individual places. Outside was a cobbled drying area providing ample space for the washing lines.

Whoever did the washing, whether mistress, cook, maid, or laundress had a laborious job.

CHAPTER IV

Equipment and its Use

Wash on Thursday – you've your ain sel' to blame

The Copper The copper was one of the most important pieces of equipment for the laundress as it was regarded as essential to boil the white clothes. It was made of copper, as the name implies, or iron. It could be portable and kept outside under a rough shelter, as happened sometimes on farms, where it was also used on pig-killing days. More often it was bricked into the corner of the washhouse, kitchen or scullery with its own fire-box underneath and its own chimney which led sometimes into the kitchen flue. These coppers or boilers were also known as set-pots. They had their hazards, but perhaps no more so than some modern electrical equipment.

There were some problems about rust marks on the clothes, as in the *Girls Own Paper* for 1884 where a correspondence seems to have arisen on this matter:–

> *Washday* must clean the copper with bath-brick and water. It has probably been much neglected.
> *Martha,* we know of no method of helping you about the iron boiler, unless you can boil the clothes in a bag.

However, relief is at hand:–

> *Little Poll* has seen our answer to *Martha* about her troublesome rusty iron boiler, and very kindly written to say that the difficulty may be got over by white-washing the boiler with lime. Wipe the boiler dry after using it, and then white-wash it well with the lime whitewash. By the time it is next wanted it will be thoroughly dry and set, and will only cause a little hardness to the water. It must be white-washed occasionally. We thank *Little Poll* for her ready help and kindly letter.

Alas, we are never to know if Martha did or did not white-wash the boiler AND if she did – did it work!

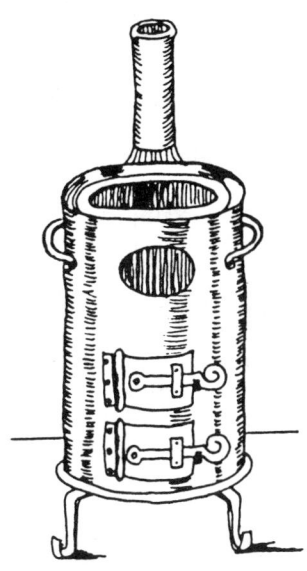

Smith & Paget, Crown Works, Keighley, made portable boilers of wrought-iron or cast-iron respectively costing £2 8s.0d for a six gallon boiler with legs and no wheels or with wheels for £3 0s.0d. The cast-iron, six-gallon boiler with a plain pan was £2 10s.0d, with rustless pan £2 17s.6d. The galvanised iron cover was 8s.0d extra. The Harrods Catalogue *Victorian Shopping* quotes 22s.0d for a six gallon galvanized boiler. One old gentleman told me with evident pleasure that their boiler was also used for boiling the Christmas puddings.

Boilers persisted until well into the 1930's, but by the early 1920's the gas boiler was the thing. To be sure, it still had to be filled by hand, but there was a tap for emptying it and Oh! the relief of lighting the gas underneath to heat the water quickly and cleanly! No more rising very early to get the copper-fire going! Electric boilers were also coming into use and the way was being paved for today's washing machines.

No boiler was complete without wooden tongs or a boiler stick to lift the hot clothes out of the water.

The Mangle Like most processes associated with washing, removing the water had always been hard work. 'Wrenching' or wringing by hand was not very successful and the later idea of rolling sheets on to a wooden roller and pressing this with a mangling board or bat still required a lot of energy. The invention of the mangle in the early part of the nineteenth

11

century was a big step forward. In 1884, many Keighley firms such as Watson & Whalley, Eagle Works; Smith, Marks & Co., Britannia Ironworks; Whalley, Smith & Paget and many others were all making mangles.

There were two main types: The Box Mangle and The Roller Mangle. The Box Mangle was to be found in large houses and the new laundries. The one at Shugborough Hall in Staffordshire, for example, was in use until the 1920's and there is an account of a new laundry in the *Yorkshire Gazette* on 12th March 1885 . . . 'Yesterday we were afforded the pleasure of seeing the new Sanitary Steam Laundry in Aldwark in full working order . . .' In the laundry was a mangle of the old pattern, the box of which was 5 feet long and 2½ feet wide, set in a strong frame and containing about 1½ tons of large stones used to press the linen. This could be moved backwards and forwards by turning a handle. Wooden rollers were supplied with the mangle and these rested under the box. In use, the mangle was placed next to a clean wooden table. On to this was put a wet sheet folded in half lengthwise and on top of this other flat pieces of linen. The whole was wound carefully round a wooden roller and covered with a piece of holland, usually supplied by the manufacturer. When the handle was turned, the mangle moved ponderously forward and at a certain stage an ingenious mechanism forced it to tilt slightly so that there was enough space to insert a roller under it. The action was continuous and the mangle moved backwards and forwards tilting first at one end and then the other, enabling the laundrymaids to take out or put in filled rollers as required.

There are accounts of the sheets and heavy items being put on the frame under the box and the rollers rolling over these, so it is possible that both methods were used. In both cases, the weight was such that nearly all the water was pressed out and the sheets only needed airing off. Imagine the back-breaking effort required to get those stones moving!

These mangles are still remembered by old people who have used them. One countrywoman told me how a cottage kitchen was dominated by such a monster. The proud owner did the mangling for the whole village, thereby earning a few pence for doing so. The family skirted the immense object warily. An old man remembered the indignity of being sent every Monday with a basket of wet clothes to have them mangled. 'Not suitable' he said 'for a *boy* to be seen doing such a thing'. In the cities it was quite usual to see a notice saying: *Mangling done here.*

The roller mangles were large solid affairs consisting of two, sometimes three, wooden rollers set in an upright metal frame. The pressure on these was supplied with a metal screw and they were turned by a handle. In the better mangles the bottom roller was made of Lignum Vitae, a very hard wood. As in the case of the poss-stick, the village carpenter would set aside suitable pieces of wood for rollers, as it was quite usual to have new rollers made by him when the others wore out. These mangles stood foursquare on sturdy metal legs which were often ornate and usually on wheels. Those with three rollers could be used rather like a linen press as damp tablecloths could be rolled on to the centre roller and left there for some time. They emerged from this ordeal flat and shiny and requiring little ironing to finish them.

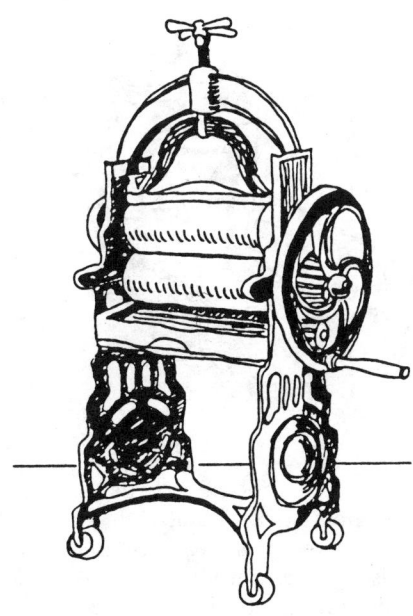

Some mangles were supplied with a wooden tray which helped to support the heavier items passing through the rollers. Often two people worked the mangle: one fed the sheets into the rollers and the other turned the handle. This could be hazardous, as a sudden careless increase in speed on the part of the turner could mean a finger or hand caught between the rollers. There are still people bearing the scars of such an accident to this day.

There is a rather alarming reference to a mangle in *The Heyday* by Bamber Gascoigne, reprinted here by kind permission of Curtis Brown:

> And in the laundry she was even more amazed by the mangle, turned by a long pole which had interchangeable leather fittings for three kitchen maids or one horse. It was made locally and still sits there, rusting slowly away.

The mind boggles at the thought!

The large mangle was gradually superseded by the small wringer with rubber rollers which could be attached to the wash-tub or the early type of hand-operated washing machine. In the 1920's and 30's free-standing models were available which were much easier to use and took up far less space.

Rubbing Board The first rubbing boards, or wash boards, were of wood and, like the poss-stick, made by the local carpenter. The prototypes were there in the washing bats used earlier. One Victorian example I have seen is about a foot wide and has a neat concave curve to accommodate the figure. There is a ledge for soap and wooden corrugations on the board itself, the whole being tailored to fit into the

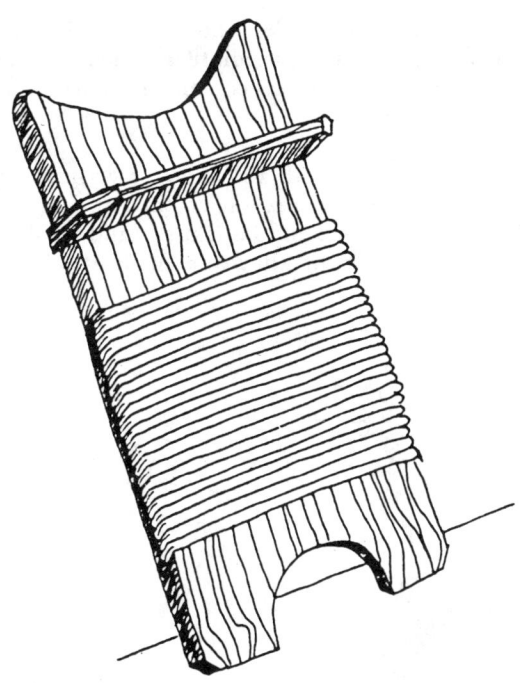

washing tub or sink. Those manufactured by such firms as Smith & Paget at the Crown Works, Keighley, had a strong wooden frame with corrugations of fluted zinc, tin or glass. The tin and zinc were durable, but apt to wear the clothes. Glass gave a good rubbing surface, but could be broken easily either by a fall or too hot water.

Tubs   Tubs were of good seasoned oak, oval or round or in the shape of a trough with a flat bottom and sides sloping outwards. These were placed on a table or stand so that they were the right height for the user. Water had to be kept in these at all times otherwise the wood dried and shrank and they leaked. There is an amusing story about a complaint from a large and prestigious house to the firm which had supplied the tubs for the new washhouse – 'they leaked, were useless etc.' A member of the firm was sent post-haste to investigate and quickly righted the wrong by standing the tubs in the horse trough!

Towards the end of the century and up to World War I, steel or zinc dolly tubs became popular and gradually the old tubs were burnt or used for pleasanter purposes such as growing flowers. The zinc tubs were corrugated, some had soap holders and a pouring lip so the water didn't splash so much when the tub was emptied. Others had a reinforced thick rim at the top so that the water was contained when the clothes were being possed or dollied around.

Sinks Those households with a laundry or washhouse AND running water might have a slopstone sink – a flat stone or slate sink with a slightly raised edge. Here, clothes could be laid flat and scrubbed. Other sinks were similar to the tubs, in that they were made of wood, metal and then, joy of joys, porcelain.

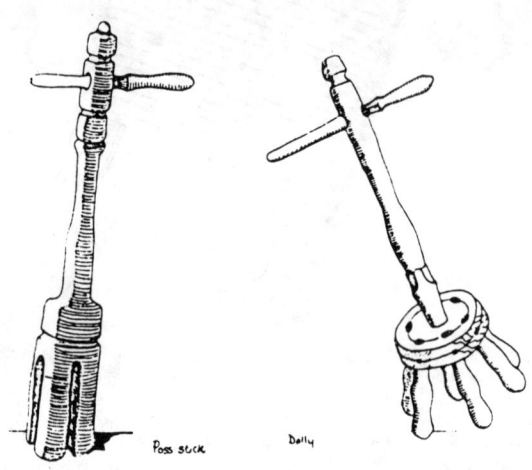

Poss stick   Dolly

The Poss-Stick and the Dolly Two essential aids to washing from the middle of the nineteenth century up to the 1930's were the poss-stick and the dolly. In fact, they are both still to be found in country districts, some yet in use for washing the odd blanket. Both pieces of equipment seem to have acquired pet names. The dolly especially is known as 'peggy', 'peggy stick', 'peggy legs', 'the maiden', 'the dolly stick' and 'the dolly maiden'. The name seems to have varied from district to district. Whatever the name, it conjures up a rather stiff little person, serious in character, willing and able to wash the clothes. It was a wooden implement like a four or six legged stool with a long handle coming from the centre, with a cross-bar. In use it was twisted and moved backwards and forwards in a dolly tub, washing the clothes by forcing the soapy water through them. A good washerwoman could get up a regular swing so that the tub danced on the washhouse floor. It was hard work though. The cross-bar was slotted into a hole in the handle and could be removed to stir the clothes in the set pot

16

or to lift them from there to the tub or sink for rinsing. It is interesting to note that in a book called *Woman's World,* printed and published by Lever Brothers Limited in 1901, the dolly is mentioned as being 'a trifle antiquated, for SUNLIGHT SOAP and LUX render its use superfluous'.

The poss-stick, or podger, was a more solid affair. Made from one piece of wood, it had a thick shank widening to a cylinder with four cuts in it. Like the dolly it had a removable cross-bar. In use it was lifted up and down in the poss-tub thumping the dirt out of the clothes in the hot soapy water. Incidentally, in the Middle Ages 'poss' meant to thrust (as with a lance); the later meaning included any kind of poking or beating as applied to washing clothes.

Very often the local joiner would make these as a wedding present, saving a good solid piece of wood for just such a purpose. It was a welcome gift.

Also in the early part of the twentieth century came the posher or posser. A bell-shaped object with holes in it made of copper, the shank could be long or short, depending on whether it was to be used in a tub or sink. When lifted up and down in the water it washed the clothes by suction.

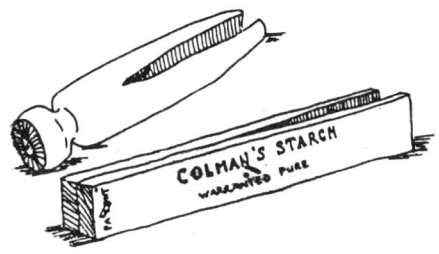

Pegs Pegs used in earlier times were of necessity larger, longer and stronger than those used today as they were required to hold heavier materials. Some were hand-turned and had shapely little heads and legs. No wonder the poorer children dressed them in bits of cloth and played with their 'dolly pegs'.

Gypsy pegs held together with a twist of tin were scorned as they had a tendency to put rust marks on the clothes.

The spring-clip arrived at the beginning of the century. No self-respecting laundry was without a peg bag, often made from a piece of blue and white striped ticking. It hung on a convenient nail or was fastened to the clothes basket.

Clothes Line   The best clothes lines were of hair but usually a good linen rope sufficed. Both pegs and line were boiled now and then. No line was without a prop, a pole pointed at one end and notched at the other to raise the line so that any breeze would help dry the clothes.

Clothes Basket   Victorian and Edwardian baskets were of willow twigs and more rectangular in shape than the later ones, which were oval. Both had sloping sides and handles.

Clothes-Horse   Then, as now, everyone hated a wet washing day. If it was necessary to dry clothes indoors a clothes-horse was put round the fire. Made of wood and having two or three leaves, it opened out like a screen. The equivalent is still used today but it is a lighter affair made of plastic.

   In the country where hedges were used to hold the clothes to be dried, those clothes-horses rejoiced in the name of 'winter hedges'.

Pulley   A pulley which hung from the ceiling was also a help. These could be six to ten feet in length and might consist of one long piece of wood or several. In Yorkshire they served a double role in the farmhouses where barley bread was made, as it was hung over the pulley to dry. Depending on where you lived, the pulley could be an airer, rack, scotch airer or creels.

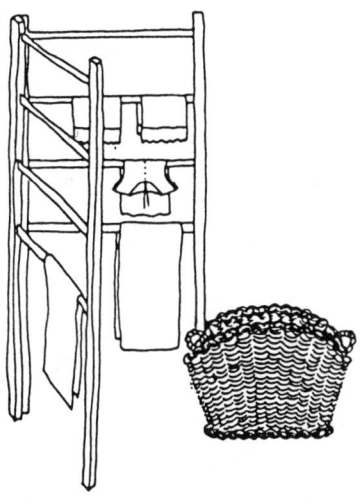

CHAPTER V

Washday

Wash on Friday – wash for need
Wash on Saturday – dirty sluts indeed

GRANDMOTHERS AND GREAT-GRANDMOTHERS have spoken to me about washdays from Edwardian times until the 1930's. There is little variation in the tale. For example, washday in the mining villages of Northumberland were almost fiendish affairs if we are to believe the old miner who declared they were 'The Devil's Birthday', and when he saw the wash-tub and mangle standing, he was glad to get out to work. Broth and Dumplings Day was another name for washday.

Often as not, the washing was done in the back yard and on Mondays, sacrosanct to washing, the noise of the poss-sticks thumping the clothes in the hot sudsy water echoed up and down the lanes like tom-toms.

The following description by a miner's wife gives some idea of what went on:–

> *Preparation* – Put all soiled whites in poss-tub, large white sheets, tablecloths etc. at the bottom, ending with doylies, tray cloths etc. Well cover with clean, cold water, leave to soak overnight. Fill the set-pot with water then add shredded bar soap, about ½lb. (No washing powder).
>
> *The following morning* – Light a fire under set-pot and while water is heating, wring out whites in tub. Sort out coloureds into piles (referred to as possings) keeping heavily soiled garments to one side.
>
> *First round* – Fill poss-tub one-third full with hot water from set-pot. Shake in cleanest whites and poss down thoroughly. Leave to soak while pot is being refilled for next round. Return to tub and poss for five minutes. Wring out smalls by hand, other linen goes through the wooden mangle. More whites are treated in the same way. Coloureds follow. End with the heaviest soiled clothes.

Second round – Refill set-pot, add more shredded soap. Shake the possed linen into set-pot and boil for twenty minutes. Smalls can be put into a pillow-case. Press the linen down with the pot stick, making sure all linen is totally immersed. Repeat this for each possing.

Third round – Lift the linen from the set-pot using boiler tongs or the pot stick. Put into a tub of cold water, poss vigorously to squeeze out soapy water. Continue with each possing.

Final round – Squeeze a little blue into cold water and poss all whites. Put through mangle. Fold, mangle again. Starch where needed. Hang on line to dry. Empty tub, take fire away from set-pot. Empty set-pot. Finish all coloureds in clean warm water. Dry all equipment with clean cloth and heave a great sigh of relief.

Another brief account written by someone whose family could afford help was as follows:–

Our family washdays were tremendous affairs. Our maid and a washerwoman supervised by the old family retainer, Nellie Henderson, carried the clothes in baskets up to the washhouse, which was situated at the end of the lane well away from the house. I wasn't allowed to go very often, but I remember the huge pot and poss-tubs with poss-sticks and large quantities of hot tea and tea-cakes consumed. They worked hard, but there was a lot of laughter and I felt they enjoyed the change from housework.

A word here about blue-ing and starching. These were important processes in the washing of white clothes, so much so that one washerwoman couldn't even start unless she was sure the blue was available. The blue, a very fine powder, was bought in small bags and most people seem to remember *Reckitts Blue* which has been purchased since 1840. It is still available. The blue bag was squeezed in the last cold

rinsing water and the laundress held the blued water in the palm of her hand. If it looked sky-blue, it was the correct colour. The blue helped to counteract any yellowness in the white clothes. One lady remembers Dolly Blue, a sort of small cotton bag, gathered round in a wooden peg, giving the appearance of a small doll from whose skirt flowed a wonderful, magical blueness!

Starch was used to stiffen such items as tablecloths, frills, doilies, aprons etc. It also gave a gloss to the clothes and helped them to keep clean longer. It was made as required by mixing with cold water to a paste, then adding boiling water until the mixture thickened and became semi-transparent. This was known as full strength starch. Such starch could be used for doilies, net curtains and caps. It was diluted as required for other items, e.g. one measure starch to four measures water for aprons.

Cold water starch was necessary for the stiff collars and shirt fronts of the day. Here the starch was mixed with cold water and left to soak for a few days to soften the starch grains before it was used. This starch was rubbed into the collars which were subsequently polished.

There are various advertisements for Blue and Starch in one of the magazines of the day – *Good Words* 1875:

Reckitts Paris Blue – as used in the Laundry of the Prince of Wales.

Colman's indigo Blue – Unrivalled for Laundry Purposes

Colman's azure Blue

Both are upstaged, however, by Glenfields :–

Glenfield Starch – is the only kind used in
Her Majesty's Laundry.

If there are any ladies who have not yet used the GLENFIELD STARCH they are respectfully solicited to give it a trial, and carefully follow out the directions printed on every package, and if this is done they will say, like the Queen's Laundress:
IT IS THE FINEST STARCH THEY EVER USED.

Whatever would they have thought of the spray starches used today!

It would be a pity not to mention here the lady whose Mother was never very well on washdays! She retreated to bed in a room above the kitchen and when possing commenced, lay and counted the number of thumps. If a hundred were not forthcoming she thumped on the ceiling!

There is also an account of washing the moleskin trousers of the men who worked in the ironstone mines :–

About one hundred years ago, the women scrubbed the moleskin trousers worn by the men with white sand. It was a case of who could turn their man out in the whitest moleskins. Then, after the washing was done, all the remaining water was used: yard, alleyway and front pavement was swilled: steps, window sills and set-pot top were sanded. Toilet seat and brush handles scrubbed. Finally, the floor cloth and line boiled. Children were bathed.

The old woman who wrote to me saying 'no need for keep-fit classes in those days' certainly had a point.

There was no great change in home washing generally until after World War II. Then technological developments in washing machines, washing powders and materials made life a great deal easier for the housewife, at least in the physical sense.

Drying

In the pit villages and back streets of the towns, washing was hung out in the back lanes. Each house had its own clothes line and prop. The housewives vied with one another to have their sheets on the line first. The lanes had their disadvantages, as coal carts were driven down them. It was an irritating day when the coal man drove through, for if you were not to be back to square one with the washing, it had to be taken down until the horse and cart with dirty coal bags had passed, and then hung up again. Also, small boys were not averse to running under and around the wet clothes, the odd sadist amongst them removing the clothes prop.

If by any chance there was an infringement in the drying space allocated to each house, rows were caused. Some women did not mince words, they just cut the line!

In the country it was easier. As well as a line of washing in the garden, the hedges would be utilised to hold towels and smaller items to dry. Indoors, on wet days, pulleys from the ceiling or clothes-horses held the clothes to be dried round the open fire.

Bigger houses had drying areas in the garden and in Scotland no self-respecting house was without a bleaching green. This was a square of grass, usually enclosed by hedges on which the whites were laid to bleach in the sun. Now and again the washerwoman would sprinkle these with fresh cold water to help on the process.

There seems to have been two different schools of thought about drying. Either the clothes were left to dry completely – and were then sprinkled or damped down for ironing; or they were brought in half-dry and folded and rolled. The latter seems more sensible.

If by now you think that enough is enough – ironing is yet to follow.

23

CHAPTER VI

Ironing

Dashing away with a smoothing iron

As MENTIONED BEFORE, there were two opinions as to how dry the clothes should be when taken in ready for ironing. One person wrote to me saying: 'Clothes had to be got completely dry, and were then laboriously damped and folded and probably mangled before being ironed. I once asked my mother why she didn't bring the clothes in when they were still just damp, but she said that the seams inside would never dry properly'. Another person pointed out that 'all the clothes were taken in when slightly damp, for mangling and ironing'.

Believe it or not, in some houses, buttons were taken off clothes before they were mangled and then sewn on again after ironing! Such ironing as was done in those days is now a lost art. The equipment required consisted of the following :–

Table   The broad wooden kitchen table was used when ironing. It was padded first with a thick piece of old blanket which in turn was covered with a piece of old sheeting, preferably without joins or seams.

Ironing Board   Until around 1905 when a folding ironing board became available, people made do with a piece of wood about four or five feet long and a foot wide. This was covered like the table. As it had no legs, it was supported by the table at one end and a kitchen chair at the other. It was clumsy to use, but it did help with the ironing of the many petticoats and chemises that went to make up the wash.

Shirt or Bosom Board   There were also shirt boards, smooth pieces of wood covered as before, eighteen inches by eleven inches in size, a little bigger than a large shirt front. These were necessary when polishing the stiff fronts.

Sleeve Boards   There are accounts of home-made sleeve boards but these were not generally in use.

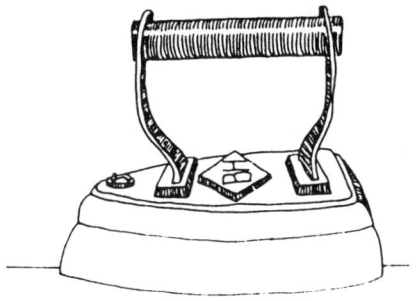

Flat Irons Flat irons were made of heavy cast iron faced with polished steel and numbered from one to ten. Oddly enough the numbers seemed to bear no relation to the weight. Number two weighing between 4-5¾ pounds was for general use, Number three was for heavy work and the very small irons were for the frills and furbelows on the children's clothes. They were heated on top of the kitchen range or in front of a good glowing fire. A shield was invented to clasp on the iron which helped to protect the clothes from any smuts from the coal.

When gas became popular these irons could be heated on a gas ring, but if so there were instructions about seeing that the iron was wiped during the heating as it sweated and moisture formed on the cold iron. This could result in rust marks on the clothes.

Iron Holder The handles of these irons became hot, so an iron holder was a necessity. It was a home-made affair of thick wool or felt with a cover of strong, washable material such as ticking. They were made into a square, then folded in two, the back end being stitched up to fit over the back of the iron handle.

Once the iron was heated, it was rubbed over bathbrick, a coarse scouring powder, wiped with a cloth and finally rubbed with a piece of soap or beeswax or candle, (kept on the ironing table in a clean linen bag), which helped the iron to glide over the clothes. The heat of the iron had to be gauged by the ironer. One method was to flick water on to it. If the water flipped off the iron, it was very hot, if it sizzled sulkily it wasn't ready. Most people spat on the irons to test them.

Polishing Iron Similar to the flat iron was the polishing iron with a convex base. It presented a smaller surface to the material, which in turn meant that there was greater pressure which gave a higher sheen to the starched collars or fronts for which it was used.

Box Irons These had been in use since the sixteenth century and were heated in a different way. The iron consisted of a hollow box shaped like the flat iron. The cavity was filled by a bolt which was heated in the fire. The following account gives some idea of their use:–

> If I had to deal with this now I should be terrified – the heater had a hole in it by which it was hooked up and lifted by a metal rod, after being heated to red-hot on the fire. The lid of the iron fastened on with a lever, one heater in the iron and another heating in the fire was the order of the day.

A Mrs Potts of Iowa, U.S.A., patented her iron in 1870. It was a box iron with a clip-on wooden handle which could be transferred from iron to iron. These handles were much better than the hot metal ones. A handle, three irons and a stand constituted a set.

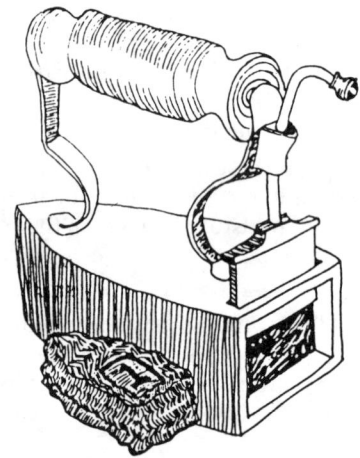

Box iron

Some box irons were filled with hot charcoal. The charcoal was heated in the fire in special containers like small rounded baskets made of wire. The iron had a funnel at the front to provide ventilation. They were very temperamental and if not properly used, great smuts would issue from them, trying the tempers of the ironers and ruining the clean washing. I have been told how in certain mill districts on a Monday evening, people came out of their houses to blow their charcoal irons to get them going. Better smuts outside than in! The glow was pretty in the dark.

Gas irons appeared between 1880 and 1890. Like the box iron, they were hollow but were heated by jets of gas conveyed to the iron by a long flexible tube. Although easy to use and regulate, some people found the tube a nuisance, (a small girl was always in trouble for tripping over it), and in the early days of gas, they tended to give off fumes.

Electric Iron   By 1894 the City of London Lighting Company produced an electric iron. To be sure it weighed fourteen pounds but it was the forerunner of today's light steam iron.

There were other flat irons in this period but those mentioned were the most usual.

Goffering Tongs or Irons   These long scissor-shaped irons were used to regulate the fulness of starched frills and laces. Frills were common on caps, bonnets, petticoats and the *best* pillowcases. Many a matron to this day bemoans the fact that they are no longer popular, as the once goffered cap badge of authority may now – Oh, the indignity! – be made of paper.

To heat the tongs, they were put on top of the stove with a flat iron to hold them down, or later they rested on a gas ring. They were tested for heat on a piece of paper – it soon became obvious if they were too hot – and then they were cleaned with a duster. In use, they were held like a pair of scissors with the thumb of the right hand slightly downwards. The hand was then turned towards the right while the fingers of the left kept the material over the left point of the iron. The iron was then removed and moved along and the whole repeated working from right to left. When done by an experienced hand, the results were very smart indeed but much practice was needed.

Goffering Machine   How laundresses must have rejoiced over the invention of this little machine, which came into being about the middle of the nineteenth century. It could be screwed to the table and was really a

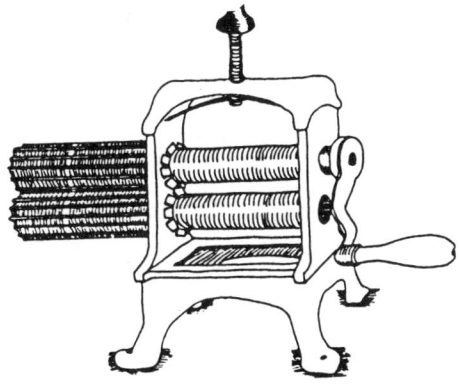

miniature wringer with corrugated brass rollers which were hollow. Hot metal bars were slipped into the rollers. The articles to be goffered were fed through the rollers; the results were crisp and even, but care had to be taken to get the material in straight, otherwise the pleats went awry.

It seems rather sad that none of these irons have nicknames like the dolly. Perhaps by the time people came to do the ironing, they were too tired for such frivolities.

When it came to the actual ironing, everyone had their own methods, but generally speaking thick seams and double parts were dried off, then all the odd pieces such as collars and cuffs and, finally, the plain parts were done.

Laces and embroideries were pressed on the wrong side over a thick piece of flannel so that the pattern was pushed into the flannel and consequently stood out when dried. Ironing on the right side gave a sheen or gloss, table napkins would be done thus. Ironing on the wrong side gave a dull finish.

Everything had its correct fold so that when completed and aired they could be put away tidily. In the well-organised linen cupboard or linen press, garments, towels etc. could be checked and counted at a glance.

With the change in fabrics and washing methods today, ironing is no longer necessary and many of the liberated young do not bother to iron at all. They are, however, both impressed and horrified when confronted in some of Britain's stately homes by these memories of Monday.

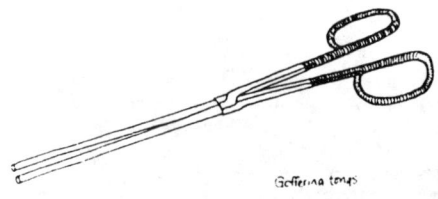

Goffering tongs

CHAPTER VII

Payment for Washing

PAYMENT FOR LAUNDRYWORK SEEMS LOW, but the wages were in line with those of the other servants. In the houses which could afford to keep a laundrymaid permanently employed, the upper laundrymaid averaged £14 a year and the under laundrymaid £10.

The sociologist Henry Mayhew in his work *London Labour and The London Poor* wrote that in 1862 a laundress would deal with the washing for a family of six for 8½d a week, inclusive of the cost of a 1lb bar of soap, soda, starch and coal.

Towards the end of the nineteenth century, laundries were being opened by private companies. At first they were rather suspect as the responsible housewife felt it was not 'de rigeur' for her clothes to be washed alongside those of other people. As servants became scarce, due in part to the 1914/18 war when many women went into munitions, laundries gained in popularity and reassuring accounts in local papers won people over. One local paper states

> . . . the garments are thoroughly purified by having steam forced through them . . .
> . . . there are irons many and ironers not a few to carry out the indispensable work which only the hands of women can perform . . .
> . . . the baskets by which the things are brought in, as well as the books which it is necessary for the customer to keep being supplied by the company . . .

Mr H. Walsh wrote a rather pompous book on Domestic Economy in 1889 wherein he stated: 'No one would willingly encounter all the disagreeables of washing day and therefore if it were possible to obtain the services of a regular laundress out of the house on anything like the same terms as at home, many masters [note] and mistresses too would avoid a great deal of discomfort'.

Such a remark nowadays would bring howls of retribution on Mr Walsh's head. He seems the original male chauvinist pig. He goes on to suggest a bargain be struck with the laundress, either she is paid by the year or by the piece. If by the year, a family of six plus two servants might pay her £40 – a little more in London and a little less in the country. This amount is calculated under their separate heads of house linen, family body linen and servants linen: the house linen and servants linen £5 each; body linen of the family £5 a head.

Washing by the piece sets out the payment for each article. The following list is interesting as it shows the garments worn and household linen at that time:–

Counterpanes	1s.6d	Gentlemen's shirts	3d-6d
Pair of sheets	6d	Gentlemen's nightshirts	3d
Servants sheets	4d	Gentlemen's nightcap	¾d
Pillow case	1d	Gentlemen's collar	¾d
Blankets	9d-1s	Drawers	2d
Towel	¾d	Lady's muslin dress	6d-1s
Window Blind	1d	Lady's dressing gown	6d-1s
Toilet cover	1d	Lady's collar	2d
Tablecloth	3d	Sleeves per pair	2d
Tablecloth large	4d	Handkerchief	½d
Tablenapkin	1d	Frills	1d
Kitchen cloths	9d	Habit shirt without collar	1d
Couvrette	1d	Petticoat	3d
		Baby's petticoat	1d
		Chemise	2d
		Drawers	2d
		Stockings	1d
		Nightgown	3d
		Nightcaps	1½d-3d
		Flannel petticoat	2d
		Children's clothes by the dozen	8d-10d
		Stockings	1d
		Handkerchief	½d
		Flannel waistcoat	2d

Washing by the dozen – a sum of 1s.0d is quoted unless blankets, sheets, large tablecloths and gentlemen's shirts are included. When included, 1s.3d is the sum mentioned.

When looking for records of such payments I paged through the accounts in the York Minster library but found little of interest until 1904, when a Mrs Green was paid £1 3s. 9d for washing dusters etc., followed in August by 16s.3d for washing towels.

October 1914 shows Mrs Prime who, for the Dean and Chapter, from 4th August till 26th October, was paid for washing :–

59 towels	(1d each)	4s.11d
186 dusters	(½d each)	7s.9d
2 dust sheets	(4d each)	8d

Was there an autumn cleaning of the Minster that so many dusters had been in use?

In the 1920's, some of these laundries would do a bag-wash where garments were returned to the customer clean, but not ironed. Quite a large bag was done for 2s.9d, but it was pointed out to customers that the washing was not hand-finished.

It was still hard work for the women in the laundries, who put in a twelve-hour day, and in one laundry on the borders brought their babies with them – no doubt leaving them asleep, safe in a clothes basket, while they worked.

The wheel turns and the heyday of the laundries is over. The washing machine and drier have seen to that and in the towns the Washetaria reigns. Round go a motley selection of clothes for 90p while their owner gossips, reads or shops. The only effort required is to press a button or two and add the soap powder.

CHAPTER VIII

Laundry Recipes

THE VICTORIAN/EDWARDIAN HOUSEWIVES had their own pet recipes for laundrywork. Many of these derived from their kitchen supplies and the following are just a sample:–

Alum Water   Used for rinsing curtains and muslin hangings and children's dresses and pinafores, rendering them non-flammable.

> *Dissolve two ounces in one gallon of water, and use for rinsing.*

Borax   Is a valuable cleaning and bleaching agent.

> *The proportion is one tablespoonful of Borax to one gallon of water. Boil a little of this water, dissolve the Borax in it, and then add the remainder before placing the linen in it.*

Borax is also used to give lace a slight stiffness. Use two teaspoons of Borax dissolved in half a pint of water.

Bran Water   Used for cretonne, chintz, crewel work, canvas and holland. It cleans and stiffens the fabrics and preserves the colour.

> *1 part of Bran*
> *4 parts of Water*
> *Measure the amount of bran and water required into an old pan. Bring to the boil, simmer 30 minutes. Strain. Repeat using the same bran and fresh water. Strain and mix the two solutions. Use this without soap for washing and rinsing the materials.*

Another recipe suggests:

> *1 pound of bran to a gallon of boiling water. Prepare overnight and use the clear part, tepid, the next morning for washing and rinsing the crewel work.*

Bran is also advocated for cleaning white woollen shawls. The bran is heated in the oven or by the side of the stove and then rubbed gently into the shawls.

Coffee   Use strained coffee when rinsing net or sleeves, if a cream colour is required. If too strong the materials thus treated have a faint smell of coffee.

Gin	Is a help in removing some stains. (It was very much cheaper then than it is today!)
Gum Arabic	A solution of the gum is made and used for the slight stiffening of chiffon, ribbon, fine silk, lace, veilings and crepes.

Gum Water

2 oz Gum Arabic
½ pint of boiling water
Crush the gum, put it into a basin and pour boiling water over it. Stir and when dissolved, strain through a fine cloth into a jug. Bottle.

Javelle Water A mixture of chloride of lime and washing soda, an efficient bleach. It must never be used for woollens or silk.

8 oz soda   4oz chloride of lime
1 pint water   1 quart water
Put the soda into a basin and add boiling water. Mix the lime with cold water. Mix the two solutions by stirring with a stick.
Once the mixture has settled and is clear, bottle the clear liquid. Keep in a dark place. To remove stains from white clothes, use equal quantities of Javelle water and warm water. Rinse well.

Milk Warm milk was often advocated for the removal of ink stains.

Onion Many a white garment was scorched through using too hot an iron and the following recipe is given in a book on Elementary Laundrywork published in 1901:

Scorch Mixture
1 onion   ½ pint vinegar
2 oz washing soda   2 oz fullers earth
Peel slice and pound onion to extract the juice. Add the other ingredients to the juice. Put the mixture in a bottle. Spread a little over the scorched part and allow it to get quite dry. Repeat until the mark disappears.
Quite a witches brew!!!

Potato Potatoes yielded starch. Either the potato water was used for stiffening, after they had been boiled, or the potatoes were grated coarsely in water and left to stand. The water was drained off and the deposit dried.

Rice Like the potato, rice also produces starch and the water it is boiled in can be used for stiffening. The starch manufactured commercially from rice is considered of very fine quality.

Saffron	Is used for tinting muslin and lace.
Salt	Is used to set colours.
	Dissolve one tablespoonful of salt in each quart of rinsing water. If wine or fruit has been spilt on the tablecloth, sprinkle at once with salt and wash as quickly as possible afterwards.
Sugar	*12 lumps to a tea-cup of water for stiffening lace and doilies.*
Tea	Like coffee, strained tea is sometimes used for tinting. It is preferred to coffee as it leaves no smell and is a clear solution.
Vinegar	Put into the cold rinsing water, it prevents colour from running.

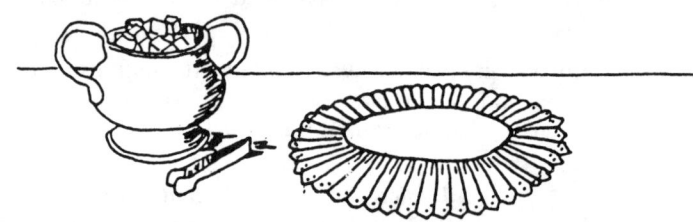

CHAPTER IX

Washing Machines

SURELY THE FIRST WASHING MACHINES were greeted with relief by the laundresses of the day. Of course, the inevitable wet blanket suggested that home washing could be easily done without these. Such virtuous remarks were usually made by those who had no idea of the work involved.

As the nineteenth century gave way to the twentieth there came a surge of inventions to the aid of the laundress. The first washing machines were hand-operated and still required a good deal of effort. One was based on our old friend the dolly. A handle was turned and the dolly revolved in the centre of the tub which contained soap, hot water and the dirty clothes. The friction and agitation cleaned them.

In 1862 came a watertight box, fitted to rockers like a rocking horse and fitted inside with corrugated boards. The box was filled with water, soap and the washing and then the lid was put on. The laundress rocked it up and down to provide the motion required to loosen the dirt.

In their 1884 catalogue, Whalley Smith and Paget of Keighley advertised Wringers, Mangles and Sewing Machines. A washer is shown which consists of a tub with an agitator fixed to the mangle above and turned by a gear handle.

Other machines, working on the principle of the rubbing board, cleaned the clothes by friction. In these the rotating wooden disc was corrugated, as was part of the washer. As the handle turned the disc, the clothes were rubbed between the two grooved pieces of wood. One such was in use in 1914 and can be seen in Beningbrough Hall in Yorkshire.

Another still used in the 30's had four wooden paddles which moved when the handle was turned. It also had a small rubber wringer which was an improvement on the heavy mangle. It was quite hard work to use.

It was not until the 1920's that electricity was harnessed to mechanise the washing machine. I well remember seeing our first such. It was an enamelled tub which stood firmly on its four legs in our washhouse. Inside

35

were four metal cones attached to a central lever which both pressed the cones down onto the clothes and then lifted them away. The clothes were cleaned by pressure and suction.

We have come a long way with washing machines since then. Whether the satisfaction gained when our washday is done is as great now as it must have been to our forebears is a matter for debate.

CHAPTER X

Mair Memories of Monday

AFTER THIS BOOKLET WAS PUBLISHED, letters came from Scotland about Highland Washing. Although many methods were the same as those of the Sassenachs, there were some differences and these have been amalgamated into this chapter.

In the country

Often, on the farms in the Highlands there was no washhouse and the clothes were boiled in a big pot, on an outside fire, the pot resting on bricks or stones. I have a postcard depicting this dated 1910. Pleasant enough on a warm, sunny day but just imagine the difficulties with a sulky fire or one roaring away when the wind blew. If the farm was near the sea the same pot might also be put to other uses, such as boiling 'Buckies' better known perhaps as whelks.

The most delightful description of a country washhouse over 60 years ago came in a letter from Glamis –

Granny's washhouse was a lean-to built on to the rear wall of her cottage. It had a wooden floor and a window which looked out to the burn. There was a fire-place built on to the rear wall of her cottage and on it were two, huge, black pots to boil the water. The water was carried from the burn by the bucketful. It was years after the Great War till a boiler, enclosed in brick, was built into the washhouse and still the water was carried from the burn.

The letter tells also of the fun of tramping blankets, a method popular in Scotland for over 200 years.

On warm, sunny days the children would be playing barefoot in the garden when their Mother would carry a tub outside filled with blankets and warm, sudsy water. With whoops of delight, they hopped into the tub and pranced about, pushing the soapy water through the blankets, thereby loosening the dirt. After rinsing, neighbours all helped by taking a corner of the blanket and shaking it up and down to remove the water until it made a cracking sound like gunshot. Afterwards, drying under the trees on the green, how sweet and fresh the blankets smelt.

Letters from others who had been in service on farms, told how they and the mistress tramped the blankets and old cards and pictures show that clothes received the same treatment. The ladies illustrated have their skirts and petticoats hitched up or tucked into their very, respectable, looking knickers. The message on the back of one of the cards reads 'This is how the lassies wash in Glasgow'. The datemark is 1904, others are between 1904–1908.

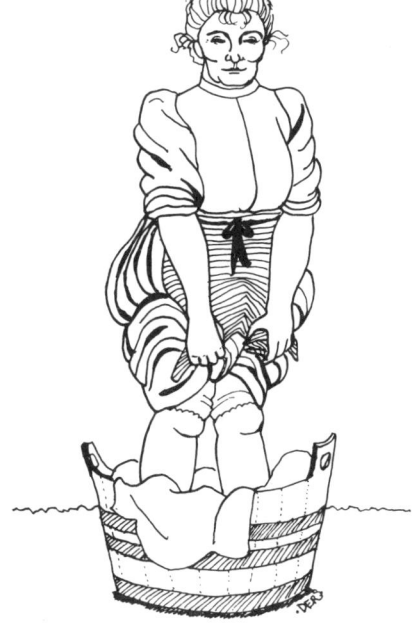

In the town

In the 1920's a rented house in town, one of a block of four had the use of a shared washhouse and drying green. The factor, an agent appointed to look after the running of the houses, allocated a washday for each family. The night before, clothes were collected, sorted and soaked, the family wringer fixed into place and the boiler fire set. The door was then locked and the key taken inside. Early next day the usual exhausting process began. Sometimes neighbours with large families asked that a little hot water be left so that they could rub a few things through to keep going as it were. At the end of the day it was a matter of pride to leave the washhouse clean and well scrubbed for the next family.

From towns like Edinburgh and Glasgow came tales of the 'Steamies', the affectionate name given to the Public Washhouses. What a godsend they were to those living in the high tenements and small cramped houses in the closes, none of which had hot water. The information from a group of 'oldies' in their 70's and 80's talking on tape of their weekly visit to one of them is an eye-opener. All agreed that you collected your soap powder, A1 and Babbits were the favourites, and bundled up your washing. If you had a pram or go-cart you put it in there and pushed it along to the Steamie. Otherwise you humped it there or took a bus. There you paid your money at the door, entered and once inside had the use of unlimited hot water, a type of spin-drier, mangle, a drying cupboard and irons. One or two people said darkly that unless you watched the drying cupboard a lot of pilfering went on, especially at Christmas time.

As well as getting through the washing you had a crack or gossip with your friends as already mentioned in Chapter III. One lady always dressed up for the Steamie as it was a social occasion. Another said you could always tell who had been there as they were all pink and smelt of washing.

Once home, the clothes were aired on a pulley. Everyone seems to have had one, either in the kitchen, or along the passage to the door. If clothes had to be dried, in the tenements there were clothes ropes on pulleys worked from the kitchen window. The washing flapped outside the window and could be a nuisance as it twined on the ropes making them difficult to pull in.

I see that the trendy magazines are advertising beautiful wooden pulleys to embellish your home, so once again the wheel turns.

Three interesting words cropped up, a luggie, a pin and rizzard. A luggie is a ladle, a pin a bundle. Clothes were rizzard when half dried. These words are to be found in the Oxford Dictionary but are no longer in common use where washing is concerned.

One last tale of the tub. Many years ago I taught in a Scottish school. The laundry was a makeshift affair but it boasted six sinks. On my first day there I discovered if one stopper was pulled out, all the others plopped out at the same time. The great cry in our lesson was always 'Haud yer stoppers' so now I'll haud my whisht.